D1549678

01. DEC

250 471 679

WORKING STEAM
Gresley V2s

Gavin Morrison

Introduction

The first example of Sir Nigel Gresley's Class V2 design for the LNER, No 4771 *Green Arrow*, entered service in 1936, having been built at Doncaster Works as 24 other members of the class would be; the remainder were Darlington products. It was July 1944 when No 3695, the last to be built, emerged from Darlington, bringing the class total to 184 locomotives.

Designed for mixed-traffic duties, the 'V2s' soon proved capable of handling anything from prestige main-line express to humble pick-up freight. They were fast, handsome (especially when coupled to standard tenders with capacity for 4,200gal of water and 7½ tons of coal — locomotives attached to tenders with stepped coping and low fronts had a more old-fashioned appearance) and very strong. They were never seen on Great Eastern lines south of March, but otherwise they could be found all over the Eastern and North Eastern regions, as well as on the ex-North British main lines in Scotland. Those of us that can remember them at work on the East Coast main line recall how often they used to turn up on express diagrams where a Pacific was to be expected. This used to upset me in the 1940s and '50s, when my parents used to take me to watch the trains at Pilmoor, 16 miles north of York, but the sight and sound of these locomotives being driven hard (at up to 80mph) on heavy trains is still a vivid memory. Similarly, expresses on the Great Central main line, such as

the 'Master Cutler' and 'South Yorkshireman', will long be associated with the 'V2s', as will the main-line workings between Edinburgh and Aberdeen, which some locomotives worked for their entire careers.

Apart from the eight fitted with double chimneys, the locomotives altered little in appearance, the only really noticeable change being the outside steam pipes on those that received separate cylinders in place of the original monobloc castings. The six members of the class fitted with Kylchap cowl and double chimney in the early 1960s became known as 'super' 'V2s' and were almost the equal of Pacifics, but these changes came too late, as Type 4 diesels were already appearing on the East Coast main line.

The class did not enjoy a particularly long life, there being only 30 years between the appearance of *Green Arrow* and the withdrawal of No 60831; indeed, some of the newer members of the class managed only 20 years' service. Happily *Green Arrow* was saved for posterity by the National Railway Museum and is currently working on the national rail network, delighting all those who travel behind her, as well as lineside observers. It is to be hoped that the locomotive will continue in active service for many years to come.

Gavin Morrison
August 2002

Acknowledgements

Unfortunately good colour slides of the class in the BR lined black livery are few and far between, so the album shows the class predominantly in BR Brunswick green, plus the preserved *Green Arrow* in LNER apple green.

As always, my grateful thanks go to the photographers who have allowed me to use their slides; it was a delight to see the originals, especially those developed from Kodachrome 25ASA film.

The information for the captions has been obtained mainly from the excellent publications Yeadon's *Register of LNER Locomotives, Volume 4* and the Railway Correspondence & Travel Society's *Locomotives of the LNER, Part 6c*.

Finally, readers may like to know that a comprehensive selection of black & white photographs can be found in *The Power of the V2s*, published by Oxford Publishing Co in 2001 and still in print.

First published 2002

ISBN 0 7110 2884 2

© Ian Allan Publishing Ltd 2002

Published by Ian Allan Publishing

an imprint of Ian Allan Publishing Ltd, Hersham, Surrey KT12 4RG.
Printed by Ian Allan Printing Ltd, Hersham, Surrey KT12 4RG.

Code: 0211/B2

Title page: 'V2s' could be seen on anything from top-link express duties to humble goods trains. In 1964 No 60822 passes along the clifftops near Stonehaven, with the North Sea in the background. It spent all its 27 years allocated to either Aberdeen Ferryhill or Dundee, so it must have passed this spot hundreds of times. Not looking in the best external condition, it would be withdrawn on 7 December 1964 and cut up at Motherwell Machinery & Scrap Co at Wishaw in February 1965. *M. Mensing*

Right: A fine study of No 60972 ready to leave Aberdeen with an up express. Note the Royal Mail van on the left. Built in 1943, the locomotive went new to Eastfield shed in Glasgow and then spent the rest of its career at the ex-North British main-line sheds. It was withdrawn on 29 November 1963 from Aberdeen Ferryhill, where it had been allocated since 2 January 1956, and was sent to Inverurie Works for cutting-up.
J. W. Armstrong Trust

Left: Allocated to Top Shed, King's Cross, from 1955 to 1963, No 60902 is seen in immaculate condition at the depot on 27 January 1957, just three weeks after it has returned to service after a general repair. It was an Eastern Region locomotive throughout its career, beginning and ending its days at Doncaster. It was condemned on 22 September 1963 and cut up at Doncaster Works during November 1963. *T. B. Owen*

Above: Eight 'V2s' were fitted with double blastpipes and chimneys, but only six received the Kylchap cowl, which made them into super 'V2s' equal in performance to the 'A3' Pacifics, if not quite up to the 'A1s' and 'A4s'. Nos 60817 and 60963 were the two that received only the double blastpipe and chimney, which in itself apparently did little to improve the steaming of the locomotives, which were suffering from poor coal quality in the late 1950s. No 60817 was modified in March 1960 and is at the platform end at King's Cross, waiting to back out to Top Shed for servicing after working an up express on 18 August 1962. It was a New England locomotive at the time, and its external condition was typical for that shed around the early 1960s. *G. Rixon*

Above: Pioneer 'V2' No 60800 *Green Arrow* at Top Shed (King's Cross), where it was allocated for its entire career of 26 years, except for one month at Woodford Halse in 1953. It received its last general repair in January 1960 before being withdrawn for preservation on 21 August 1962. Now part of the National Collection, it is based at York, where it can normally be seen when not hauling specials on the main line, and is currently painted in BR Brunswick green. *R. C. Riley*

Right: In fine external condition, as was normal for the Top Shed (King's Cross) 'V2s', No 60854 heads an up goods past Finsbury Park, framed by five gantries and the signalbox. The date is 14 April 1962. New from Darlington Works on 19 April 1939, it was allocated to New England, where it ended its career 24 years later, on 16 June 1963. It spent all its time allocated to the southern end of the Eastern Region, aside from a six-month spell on the Great Central in 1957. It received its last general repair in January 1962, three months before this picture was taken. *G. Rixon*

Below: No 60909 heads an up express near Potters Bar on 13 August 1960, having reached the summit of the six-mile climb from Hatfield, the last 12 miles to King's Cross being mainly at 1 in 200 down the bank. Grantham, where it was allocated at the time, was obviously short of cleaners. This locomotive was new on 4 May 1940 to Doncaster shed, from where it was eventually withdrawn on 8 June 1962, having spent all its time at either King's Cross or Doncaster, aside from four months at Grantham in 1960. Its last general repair was at Darlington Works in November 1959. *K. L. Cook/ Rail Archive Stephenson*

Right: New England's No 60845 heads south near Potters Bar on an up parcels train on 31 August 1961. This locomotive was sent to Swindon test plant in May 1952 for steaming trials. After many difficulties — not least when it broke loose whilst on the plant at speed, resulting in damage to the cab, when it came into contact with the testbed platform — road tests were eventually carried out in February 1953 on the Great Western main line between Reading and Filton. The trials saw the locomotive attain the incredible feat of hauling 761 tons (25 coaches) for 68 miles at an average speed of 64½mph, with a maximum of 77mph being reached. After its return to the Eastern Region it spent its days allocated to Grantham and to New England, from where it was withdrawn on 23 September 1962 and sent to Doncaster Works for cutting-up. *D. Marriott*

Below: Light work for No 60821 as its races through Hadley Wood at the head of the 4.40pm King's Cross–Peterborough on 12 August 1961. Its external condition gives a good clue that it was allocated to New England shed. Apart from 21 months at St Margarets shed in Edinburgh, it was always allocated to the southern end of the East Coast main line. New to traffic on 3 December 1937 as LNER No 4792, it was one of the class to receive its number (721) allocated under the LNER's abortive early-1946 renumbering scheme, before becoming No 821 on 26 May 1946 and eventually BR 60821 on 16 April 1948. It survived until 29 December 1962. *K. L. Cook/ Rail Archive Stephenson*

Right: King's Cross-allocated No 60914 heads a down freight near Brookmans Park on 14 July 1959. At Top Shed since 1946, it moved on to New England two months after the photograph was taken. Having received its last general repair in May 1960, the locomotive would be condemned on 23 September 1962 and cut up at Doncaster Works during December. *T. B. Owen*

Left: A classic picture of No 60800 *Green Arrow* taken near Brookmans Park on 30 August 1961 on what was probably the afternoon King's Cross–Niddrie freight. It was this service upon which the locomotive had started its career (in 1936) and upon which the class operated with such success. By 1961, however, this working was often allocated to one of Top Shed's 'A4' Pacifics. As it turned out, *Green Arrow* would have only another year in traffic, before passing into preservation at the National Railway Museum in 1962. Currently it can be seen on the main line in this livery, having run in LNER apple green since it re-entered traffic back in 1973. *D. Marriott*

Below: No 60862 passes Brookmans Park on an up fitted freight on 28 February 1959, during its 13 years (1950-63) allocated to Top Shed. During a general overhaul at Darlington in October 1961, it became one of what were known as the 'super' 'V2s', when it was fitted with a Kylchap double blastpipe and chimney, which greatly improved the performance, but sadly it was withdrawn only 20 months later on 16 June 1963. Only six of the class received this modification, which came too late, as Type 4 diesels were appearing in large numbers by this time. *T. B. Owen*

Left: A picture which I feel typifies a 'V2' at work. No 60906 of New England, in terrible external condition but probably in good mechanical order, heads an up fitted freight on the fast line near Brookmans Park on 30 August 1961. New to Doncaster on 17 April 1940, it moved in November to Mexborough, where it stayed for nearly five years. There followed five years at Doncaster and then 13 at New England before withdrawal on 28 May 1963. *D. Marriott*

Below left: Another picture of No 60854 (see page 6), here heading an up petrol train (note the two barrier wagons behind the locomotive) near St Neots on 19 July 1962. It was allocated to Top Shed (King's Cross) at the time, having received its last general repair at Doncaster in January. Whilst at Doncaster Works in October 1952, No 60854 was selected for experiments with self-cleaning smokeboxes. Mr K. J. Cook, who was Chief Mechanical & Electrical Engineer at Doncaster but had a Swindon background, was persuaded to fit the locomotive with a copper-capped chimney! The modification was very short-lived, as, when the locomotive was seen at King's Cross by somebody in authority, it was ordered to be removed immediately. *K. Fairey*

Right: An impressive picture of No 60871 crossing the massive Welwyn Viaduct on 14 April 1962. For years this structure has been the main cause of the bottleneck on this section of the East Coast main line, as it carries only two lines. No 60871 was a Top Shed locomotive at the time of the photograph, but it was subsequently transferred to New England and then Doncaster before being withdrawn on 22 September 1963. Earlier in its career it had briefly carried the number 771 under the LNER's abortive early-1946 renumbering scheme. *T. B. Owen*

Left: No 60964 *The Durham Light Infantry* looks in fine external condition for a Gateshead 'V2' at the head of an up express climbing the 1 in 200 just south of Hatfield on 13 May 1961. It was new to Heaton in January 1943 but stayed only until March, when it was transferred to Gateshead. The last member of the class to be named, on 29 April 1958 by the colonel of the regiment, it is seen with the separate-cylinder modification (note the outside steam pipes), which it received at its last general overhaul in January 1960. It remained at Gateshead for 21 years, before being withdrawn in May 1964 and sent to Swindon Works for cutting-up. *D. Marriott*

Below: March shed had a small allocation of 'V2s' which were primarily used for working north, often through to York. Here we see No 60948 under repair; along with Nos 60803 and 60938 this locomotive spent eight years at the shed between 1953 and 1961. In 1961 No 60948 moved to New England, and eventually finished its days at Doncaster on 22 September 1963. This picture was taken on 2 September 1961, which was just prior to its visiting Darlington Works for its last general overhaul, when it received separately cast cylinders. *R. Hobbs*

Below: Having climbed the 15 miles of Stoke Bank on the down slow line, King's Cross-allocated No 60854 joins the double-track section at Stoke Summit and heads for the tunnel on 7 July 1962. Further details of the locomotive can be found on pages 7 and 15. *Gavin Morrison*

Right: The hard work is temporarily over for the fireman as No 60950 emerges from the north end of Stoke Tunnel with a down express after the 15-mile climb of Stoke Bank on 7 July 1962. A Grantham engine at the time (if only for five months, before moving to New England in November 1962), it was one of 71 members of the class to receive the separate cast cylinders, indicated by the outside steam pipes. *Gavin Morrison*

Left: A fine portrait of No 60871 at Grantham, waiting to take over an up express to King's Cross in September 1962. The 34A shedplate shows it was one of Top Shed's 'V2s' at the time. It spent most of its time allocated to the southern end of the East Coast main line, although it did have a spell on the Great Central in 1951/2. It was one of the six members of the class to have numberplates fixed across the upper door-strap, and lamp iron brackets mounted in a lower than normal position. It was withdrawn from Doncaster shed on 22 September 1963. *D. Penney*

Above: No 60871 as seen in the previous picture, is now leaving Grantham on the climb to Stoke Tunnel with an up express to King's Cross in September 1962. *D. Penney*

Superb winter lighting shines on No 60859 as it storms up the 1 in 178 of Gamston Bank, after the Retford stop, with a Leeds–King's Cross express on 4 January 1959. This was during its 6¾-year period allocated to Copley Hill shed. It entered traffic on 18 May 1939, and was sent new to the Great Central sheds, including Gorton, for four years. After leaving Copley Hill in September 1960 it moved to the North Eastern Region, from where it was withdrawn on 20 September 1965 from Gateshead and was sold to Ellis Metals, Swalwell, for scrapping. *D. Marriott*

An up fish train, probably from Hull, climbing Gamston Bank in fine style with No 60852 at its head. New as LNER No 4823 on 17 March 1939, this locomotive was renumbered 852 in December 1946 and was one of the last of its class to receive its BR number, being renumbered only in June 1950. It spent its entire career allocated to Doncaster, except for one month in 1946 at Copley Hill shed. Fitted with separate cylinders in October 1961 (again, one of the last to be so treated), it was withdrawn in September 1963. *D. Marriott*

Left: On 11 September 1937 LNER No 4780 was named *The Snapper — The East Yorkshire Regiment, The Duke of York's Own* (and given a fine regimental crest) at Hull Paragon station by the Colonel of the regiment. Still carrying the nameplate 25 years later as BR No 60809, the locomotive is about to enter Ashton Tunnel at the summit of Gamston Bank heading a down express. The separate cast cylinders were fitted at Darlington Works in January 1962. Allocated to the North East for its entire career, it was withdrawn from Darlington shed on 6 July 1964 and sent to Swindon for cutting-up. *D. Marriott*

Below: No 60830 makes light work of a few coal wagons as it heads south near Markham Moor in January 1963, only six months before its withdrawal from Grantham shed on 16 June 1963. As can be seen from the outside steam pipes, it was one of the 71 to receive separate cast cylinders. *D. Penney*

Left: No 60857 was new to Grantham shed as No 4828 on 10 May 1939 where it stayed for seven months before going to Doncaster. It was unusual in being allocated to Sheffield Darnall for 6½ years between March 1940 and September 1946 before returning to the Eastern Region main-line sheds. Here it is shown on an up fitted freight passing Eaton Wood on Gamston Bank on 24 June 1961. It was withdrawn from Doncaster on 17 April 1962. *D. Marriott*

Above: A fine picture of No 60809 *The Snapper* (see page 25 for further details), probably taken *c*1962, climbing Gamston Bank with at least 12 coaches behind the tender. The sound must have been fantastic. *D. Penney*

Above: No 60983 was the last 'V2' to be built, emerging from Darlington Works in July 1944. It is seen climbing Gamston Bank near Eaton Wood in fine style with an up fitted freight on 29 August 1961, during its 16 years allocated to King's Cross. It managed only 18 years of service, being withdrawn on 23 September 1962. *D. Marriott*

Right: No 60857 has already appeared on page 26, but here it is shown approaching Retford (at the bottom of Gamston Bank) at the head of a down fish train on 28 August 1961. *D. Marriott*

Left: A superb picture of No 60884 in BR lined black and with original lion-and-wheel emblem on the tender, working hard away from Retford in December 1957 on what was probably a Leeds/Bradford–King's Cross express, the locomotive then being allocated to Ardsley shed. It spent over seven years allocated to either Ardsley or Wakefield, between September 1956 and January 1964, but was withdrawn from Darlington on 6 September 1965.
D. Penney

Below: In superb winter lighting No 60862, one of the King's Cross 'super' 'V2s', crosses the River Idle just south of Retford with an up fitted freight during the winter of 1962/3. It received the Kylchap cowl and double chimney during its last general overhaul at Darlington in October 1961, but the benefits of the modification were short-lived, as it was withdrawn from New England shed in June 1963. During the LNER renumbering and the start of Nationalisation it carried the numbers 4833, 762, 862, E862 before becoming 60862, and this was in a period of just over three years. *D. Penney*

Left: This picture features another King's Cross 'super' 'V2', No 60903, as it passes the south end of Retford on an up fitted freight on 12 February 1962. This locomotive spent almost 20 of its 23 years in service allocated to Top Shed. It received the Kylchap cowl modification during its last general repair at Darlington in August 1961 but ran for just 18 months in this condition before being withdrawn from New England in February 1963. *D. Marriott*

Above: No 60876 is shown ex works from 'The Plant' at Doncaster shed during May 1956, having received a general overhaul. From December 1956 the class started to appear in BR Brunswick green. No 60876 was an Eastern Region locomotive from new (May 1940) but in November 1958 was transferred to the North Eastern Region at York, from where it was withdrawn on 19 October 1965 and sent to J. Cashmore of Great Bridge for scrapping. *J. W. Armstrong Trust*

Left: No 60872 *King's Own Yorkshire Light Infantry* was so named in Doncaster Works yard on 20 May 1939. The locomotive was unusual in that, except for two months at Grantham in 1961, it spent its entire career of 24½ years allocated to Doncaster shed, where it was photographed on 3 March 1963, six months before withdrawal. *Gavin Morrison*

Above: No 60809 *The Snapper* has already appeared on pages 24 and 27, but this time we see a rear view of it arriving at Doncaster station with a down express on 29 April 1962. The nameplate makes for easy identification. *Gavin Morrison*

Above: No 60948, one of the March-allocated members of the class, puts up a good exhaust as it leaves Gainsborough at the head of a down express on 4 October 1959. Sunday diversions were in force — still not unusual today when engineering work is taking place between Doncaster and Peterborough. Details of the locomotive appear on page 17. *D. Marriott*

Right: A very powerful picture of York's No 60887 climbing the 1-in-100 bank out of Sheffield Midland towards Dore with a mixed train on 16 November 1963. The class were quite often seen at Sheffield Midland, but sightings further south were less common. The locomotive spent all its days allocated to the main North Eastern sheds, moving on 15 September 1957 to York, from where it was withdrawn on 6 July 1964. *D. Marriott*

GREAT CENTRAL

A fine action shot of No 60899 working a Great Central express on 2 March 1963 near Charwelton. New to traffic as LNER No 4870, it put in 12 years' work at New England before moving to March for five years. Three months in mid-1957 were spent at Top Shed, before the final transfer to Doncaster, from where it was withdrawn on 22 September 1963. *M. Mensing*

MIDLAND MAIN LINE

In February 1958 the Great Central became part of the London Midland Region, and 'V2' No 60855, a Neasden engine at the time, was sent to the Midland main line to carry out clearance tests between Cricklewood and Wigston. Looking extremely clean, and with the old lion-and-wheel emblem on the tender, it is seen passing Wellingborough on 23 March 1958. Nothing came of the trials, and on 2 November 1958 the locomotive was transferred to the North Eastern Region at York, where it stayed until withdrawn on 13 April 1964. *J. Edgington*

NORTH EASTERN REGION

A portrait in Leeds Copley Hill shed yard of King's Cross 'super' 'V2' No 60903 in the usual clean Top Shed condition. The locomotive can also be seen on page 32. *Gavin Morrison*

No 60897 gets into its stride past Beeston Junction, Leeds, at the head of the 10.10 Leeds Central–Cleethorpes on 13 March 1962. A New England locomotive for most of its career, it was in fact allocated to Doncaster when this picture was taken. Withdrawal came on 11 June 1963. *Gavin Morrison*

Above left: No 60930 crosses the ex-LNWR goods yard at Wortley Junction South, on the outskirts of Leeds, at the head of an up express late in the afternoon of 31 August 1960. This locomotive put in 22 years' service, during which time it was only ever allocated to Donaster shed (36A). It was condemned on 23 September 1962 and cut up two months later in the adjacent works. *Gavin Morrison*

Left: It was unusual for the down 'Queen of Scots' Pullman to be hauled north from Leeds Central by a 'V2' in the early 1960s, as this was usually a Pacific duty. No 60848 was a Darlington engine when this picture was taken on 20 April 1960, just three weeks after its last general overhaul. New in March 1939, it was a Scottish Region engine until September 1956, when it moved from St Margarets to Gateshead. It then stayed on the North Eastern Region until withdrawn from York on 16 July 1962. *Gavin Morrison*

Above: A portrait of No 60887 in the yard at Leeds Holbeck on 6 February 1964, only five months before it was withdrawn. New in November 1939, it had spent all its time in the North East before moving to York in September 1957. *Gavin Morrison*

Left: York-allocated 'V2' No 60895 starts its journey south past Holgate station with an up freight on 4 September 1963. The racecourse station platforms can be seen on the right. No 60895 had arrived at York in July 1953 after being allocated mainly to sheds in the Newcastle area. It was withdrawn on 4 October 1965 and sent to J. Cashmore at Great Bridge for cutting-up. *D. Marriott*

Below: A well-cleaned King's Cross 'V2', No 60902, meets a very dirty 'B1' near Chaloners Whin Junction, south of York, on 22 June 1958. It is heading a fitted freight for London and will turn left at the junction to take the old main-line route to Selby. This was one of the 'V2s' to be fitted with Kylchap cowl and double chimney in October 1961. It was withdrawn in September 1963. *K. L. Cook/ Rail Archive Stephenson*

Most freights were routed around York via the avoiding lines, but a few came through the centre roads of the station. No 60946 was attached to an ex-Class D49 or J38 tender with a stepped-out coping plate, which altered its appearance considerably. It was a Thornaby locomotive at the date of the photograph (4 August 1960) and shows the liberal application of white paint to the front — a feature of Thornaby 'V2s' at this time. It was withdrawn in October 1965 and sold to Ellis Metals, Swalwell, for cutting-up. *F. J. Bullock*

The last 'V2' to be built was No 3695, which emerged from Darlington Works on 13 July 1944. New to Doncaster, it was allocated to Gorton for 19 months, from March 1945 to October 1946, but then settled down to almost 16 years at King's Cross, during which time (on 10 March 1950) it gained its BR identity of 60983. This fine picture shows the locomotive pulling away from York on the up 'Scarborough Flyer' on 25 June 1960. Note that the headboard is in place. Its last general repair was at Darlington in August 1961, and the end came on 23 September 1962, after only 18 years. *D. Marriott*

Above: Fresh from its last general overhaul at Darlington (between 8 January and 3 March 1962), No 60835 *The Green Howard* has just arrived in Clifton Yard, York, on an up freight on what was probably a running-in turn, on 17 March 1962. *Gavin Morrison*

Right: In terrible external condition, No 60839 heads south near Benningborough with an express for the London Midland Region on 22 October 1962. Apart from four months allocated to Neville Hill in 1946, it spent its 24 years at York, from where it was withdrawn on 22 October 1962. *Gavin Morrison*

Above: No 60835 *The Green Howard* was only two weeks out of Darlington Works after its last general overhaul when this picture was taken on 17 March 1962. It is heading an up freight near Benningborough, on what was probably a running-in turn. During this works visit it was fitted with a Smith speedometer and separate cylinders. A North Eastern locomotive for 25 years, on 30 June 1963 it was transferred to Aberdeen Ferryhill and put in just over two years work in Scotland before being withdrawn from St Margarets shed on 19 October 1965 and subsequently sent to G. H. Campbell at Airdrie for cutting-up. *Gavin Morrison*

Right: Still showing the white buffers and smokebox fittings which were the mark of a Thornaby 'V2' in the early 1960s, No 60885 prepares to leave Northallerton on a Darlington–Manchester express, which would travel via Harrogate and Wetherby. The 51A (Darlington) shedplate dates the photograph to after 16 June 1963, when the locomotive was transferred away from Thornaby. It survived until 6 September 1965, 3½ years after its last general overhaul, being eventually sold to Thomson's at Stockton-on-Tees for cutting-up. *J. W. Armstrong Trust*

Above: A photograph taken on 14 June 1965, the day No 60865 was withdrawn. The locomotive is seen at Darlington shed, awaiting its final journey to Ellis Metals of Swalwell for cutting-up. It spent the first 19 years on the Eastern Region, including spells at March and Copley Hill, but its final years were in the North East. The picture demonstrates how the ex-'J38' or 'D49' tender altered the appearance of a 'V2'. *Gavin Morrison*

Right: No 60809 *The Snapper* has previously featured on pages 24, 27 and 35. It had already received a casual heavy repair at Darlington in January 1962, but it would be back again in March, to sort out damage caused by a minor accident. The slightly bent front end is evident in this picture of the locomotive at Darlington shed on 12 March 1962 awaiting transfer to the works. *Gavin Morrison*

Left: A very dirty No 60806 heads south from Darlington on an up freight. The photograph was taken after October 1957, when it was fitted with separate cylinders during a general repair. A North Eastern locomotive for its 29 years of service, it achieved over 1 million miles in service. It was withdrawn in September 1966 and cut up at J. Cashmore of Great Bridge. *D. Penney*

Above: Having just emerged from its last general overhaul at Darlington Works on 12 March 1962, No 60913 stands on Darlington shed awaiting return to Heaton, its home at the time. It had been an Eastern Region locomotive until September 1958, when it moved to Tweedmouth. Records show that it had no works visits between general overhauls in May 1959 and March 1962, which is unusual. It would be withdrawn from Gateshead on 12 October 1964 and cut up at Darlington Works. *Gavin Morrison*

Left: No 60868 on shed at Darlington on 29 September 1962, having just received its last general overhaul at the adjacent works. As the shedplate (52B) indicates, the locomotive was then allocated to Heaton. It would end its days at St Margarets shed on the Scottish Region, being withdrawn four years later, on 26 September 1966, and sold to the Motherwell Machinery & Scrap Co at Wishaw for cutting-up. *Gavin Morrison*

Above: No 60809 *The Snapper* has received more than its fair share of space in this album, having already featured on pages 24, 27, 35 and 53. Here it is again, heading north through Newcastle Central station on a down freight sometime after January 1962, when it received separate cylinders. *M. Mensing*

Left: No 60922 heads south across the Royal Border Bridge with an up fish train in 1962. In the haze another train can be seen approaching, heading north past Tweedmouth. The bridge was opened in August 1850 by Queen Victoria, and was designed by Robert Stephenson and Thomas E. Harrison. It is 2,150ft in length and 126ft above the water level. No 60922 was a Heaton engine at the time but finished its days at Gateshead on 9 July 1964, being sent to Swindon Works for cutting-up in August. *M. Mensing*

Above: Gateshead's No 60976 passes north through Reston with a down express on 15 July 1961. The North British branch to Duns and St Boswells used to leave the main line here. The station was still open at this time; passenger services finished on 4 May 1964, and goods on 7 November 1966. No 60976's end came at around the same time, the locomotive being withdrawn from St Margarets shed on 26 September 1966, and despatched to Geo H. Campbell of Airdrie for cutting-up. *Gavin Morrison*

Left: Another view near Reston, this time of Tweedmouth's No 60913 heading a northbound freight during 1962. Compare this picture of the locomotive in March (page 54), when it was freshly ex works. It was withdrawn on 12 October 1964 from Gateshead shed. *M. Mensing*

Above: The easterly wind is blowing the exhaust across No 60947 as it hurries an empty fish train along the undulating gradient near Drem on 14 July 1961. This 'V2' was a Newcastle engine for 19 years before moving in September 1961 to Tweedmouth, from where it was withdrawn on 1 October 1962. *Gavin Morrison*

Below: Haymarket's No 60951 appears to be going well on an up Edinburgh Waverley–King's Cross summer relief as it passes Longniddry on 8 August 1959. The locomotive spent its entire 20-year career at either Haymarket or St Margarets. Withdrawal came on 29 December 1962, and it was cut up at Cowlairs Works the following year. *F. J. Bullock*

Right: No 60846 served three Regions during its 26-year career, ending up at St Margarets shed on the Scottish Region. Here it is seen on the shed on 18 April 1965, six months before being withdrawn and sent to G. H. Campbell at Airdrie for scrapping. This shed was rather a dangerous place, as the main line passed through it, locomotives being kept on either side. It was also a very dirty place, being in a natural depression; the air quality in the area on a Sunday evening, when locomotives were being lit up after the weekend, was horrendous. How the local residents must have rejoiced in 1967, when it closed and a modern office block was built on the site ! *R. Hobbs*

Left: Until it closed in June 1963, Carlisle Canal shed serviced those locomotives that worked over the Waverley route. Thereafter these duties were transferred to the old Caledonian Railway shed at Kingmoor, where, for a short period, it became quite normal to see both ex-LNER and ex-LMS Pacifics side by side. The picture features 'V2' No 60931, awaiting its next duty north to Edinburgh on 5 October 1963. A Scottish Region locomotive for its entire career of 24 years, it spent time at all the main-line ex-North British sheds, plus one month at Glasgow's ex-Caledonian St Rollox shed in 1960. It was withdrawn on 3 September 1965 from St Margarets and cut up at Darlington Works. *Gavin Morrison*

Below: Attached to one of the ex-Class J38 or D49 tenders, St Margarets' No 60840 comes slowly out of the cutting as it approaches Whitrope Summit after the long (11-mile) climb of almost unbroken 1 in 75 from Newcastleton on 8 July 1961. This locomotive spent its 24-year career at either Dundee or St Margarets, being withdrawn from the latter on 29 December 1962. *Gavin Morrison*

Left: No 60835 *The Green Howard* has already featured in ex-works condition on pages 49 and 57. This very fine picture shows it passing Whitrope signalbox on the Waverley route at the head of a Millerhill–Carlisle freight. The entrance to the 1,208yd tunnel is just out of sight past the brake van. The fireman will have worked hard on the 11 miles from Hawick where the gradients are mainly around 1 in 75, but the remaining 34 miles to Carlisle will be nearly all downhill. No 60835 was withdrawn from St Margarets shed on 19 October 1965. *R. Hobbs*

Above: The summit is in sight as No 60824 approaches Whitrope signalbox at the head of a freight from Carlisle to Millerhill yard in Edinburgh. The sound of a 'V2', often offbeat, battling with the 1-in-75 gradients around Steele Road and Stobs is not easily forgotten. After eight years at New England and Doncaster No 60824 moved to Scotland, where it remained until withdrawn from St Margarets shed on 26 September 1966 and sale to Motherwell Machinery & Scrap at Wishaw for cutting-up. *R. Hobbs*

Left: Shankend Viaduct is still standing about halfway between Stobs and Whitrope Summit. Just north of the station site, it has 15 arches and is 597ft long. The Waverley route closed on 6 January 1969, but the viaduct remains in the desolate surrounds as a monument to the line. The picture shows the unique 'V2' No 60813 climbing towards Whitrope over the viaduct with a Millerhill–Carlisle freight on 22 April 1965. During a general repair in 1946, as LNER No 4784, it was fitted with a stovepipe chimney and curved smoke-deflectors, which it retained until withdrawn. It had 12 years at Top Shed between December 1939 and February 1951, but then spent the rest of its career at St Margarets and Dundee. It was withdrawn on 26 September 1966 and cut up at J. McWilliam of Shettleston. *T. B. Owen*

Below: No 60883 blows off at the north end of Hawick station as it prepares to head north with a down freight in September 1958. In the background on the right is Hawick engine shed, which closed in 1966. A St Margarets engine when this picture was taken (although allocated to Newcastle for its first 17 years), No 60883's main claim to fame was that it was the only 'V2' to be repainted in LNER apple green after the war, in September 1946; it reverted to black livery at its next general repair, in July 1948. Withdrawn on 25 February 1963, it was cut up at Cowlairs Works. *D. Penney*

Left: No 60846 has already featured on page 63, but here we see it climbing the 1-in-70 gradient from Inverkeithing to North Queensferry with an up fish train in the afternoon light of 6 July 1965. *R. Hobbs*

Above: During its 28-year career No 60816 was transferred 11 times between Aberdeen Ferryhill, Haymarket and St Margarets. It is shown in the spring of 1964, leaving Perth with a full head of steam on an up express. Apparently well cleaned for a St Margarets engine, it had about another 18 months to go before being withdrawn (on 22 October 1965) and sent to G. H. Campbell of Airdrie for cutting-up. *D. Penney*

Above: No 60973 was one of the last 'V2s' built, being delivered new to Haymarket as LNER No 3685 on 27 April 1943; it was renumbered 973 in November 1946 and assumed its BR identity in May 1948. The locomotive spent all its working life based in Scotland and is seen here leaving Perth with an up express in September 1965, at which time it was allocated to Dundee. Withdrawn on 24 January 1966, it was sold for scrap to P. & W. McLellan of Langloam in March that year. *D. Penney*

Right: No 60970 was entering the twilight of its career when pictured at Gleneagles at the head of a Dundee–Glasgow service in August 1964. One of 13 members of the class to survive in Scotland (at Dundee and St Margarets) until 1966, it would be withdrawn in February of that year. Delivered new from Darlington Works in May 1943 as LNER No 3682, the locomotive was renumbered 970 in December 1946 and assumed its BR identity two years later, in December 1948. *Derek Cross*

Two pictures showing the unique 'V2' No 60813, which has already appeared on page 68.

Below: This portrait taken on Dundee shed on 6 August 1966 shows well the stovepipe chimney and small smoke-deflectors. The locomotive's immaculate external condition suggests it may recently have been on railtour duty, and it is hard to believe that it was withdrawn seven weeks later, on 26 September 1966. *D. Penney*

Right: Later the same day, immaculate No 60813 heads north near Broughty Ferry with a Blackpool–Aberdeen summer-Saturday extra. *D. Penney*

No 60970 catches the evening light on an express north of Kinnebar Junction, where the North British and Caledonian routes joined and which was the crucial point on the railway races to the North in the 1890s. No 60970 was always a Scottish Region engine, spending many years at Aberdeen Ferryhill. In 1964, when this picture was taken, it had received little external attention at St Margarets shed. This was the shed from where it was withdrawn on 7 February 1966 before being sent to Motherwell Machinery & Scrap Co at Wishaw for cutting-up. *M. Mensing*

A northbound express, believed to be headed by No 60818, is shown just north of Carmont *en route* to the next stop at Stonehaven. This locomotive had a wide sphere of operation during its career, which began at King's Cross in November 1937 and then included just over two years at Woodford Halse. It was transferred in January 1953 to St Margarets and was at Eastfield for four months in 1960. By the summer of 1964, when this picture was taken, it was allocated to Dundee, from where it would be withdrawn on 22 August 1966 and sent to Motherwell Machinery & Scrap Co at Wishaw for disposal. *M. Mensing*

PRESERVATION

Below: The pioneer 'V2', No 4771 *Green Arrow*, was selected for preservation and is the only member of the class to survive. Withdrawn on 21 August 1962 from Top Shed, King's Cross, it was stored at various locations, including Doncaster Works, Hellifield, Leicester Wigston and Preston Park, Brighton. In 1971 it became part of the National Collection and was sent to Norwich shed for restoration to working order under the capable control of Bill Harvey and his team. Its first trial run was on 28 March 1973 to Ely, and on 10 June it worked three trips from Birmingham to Tyseley; since then it has been working main-line specials, with breaks for overhauls.

Now based at the National Railway Museum in York and painted in BR Brunswick green, it is still (2002) used on specials over the national rail network.

This picture shows the locomotive on 13 September 1975 in the yard at Steamtown, Carnforth, where it was based for several years from 1973. *Gavin Morrison*

Right: Green Arrow makes a superb sight heading out of York past Clifton with a test special for Harrogate on 15 March 1978. *Gavin Morrison*

Index of Locations

Front cover: A stiff easterly wind blows the exhaust down on the up fitted freight headed by No 60902 — one of Top Shed's 'super' 'V2s' — as it passes Retford, probably during 1962. This was one of six members of the class to be fitted with Kylchap cowl and double chimney, the modification being carried out during its last general overhaul at Darlington in October 1961, but in less than two years it was withdrawn from Doncaster, on 22 September 1963. *D. Penney*

Back cover: No 60885 heads an up express near Eaton Wood on 23 May 1959, during its three-year spell (1956-9) allocated to Copley Hill shed in Leeds. This locomotive was built at Darlington, entering traffic from Heaton shed on 10 November 1939 as LNER No 4856. Withdrawal came on 6 September 1965, and it was sold for scrap the following month to Thomson's at Stockton-on-Tees. *D. Marriott*